Benchmarking Canada for Creative Comparisons – Paul Rux, Ph.D.

We can learn through comparisons. In this case, the comparisons are between Canada and the United States of America. Such comparisons can reveal benchmarks, best practices, which can benefit both countries. I know Canada first-hand. I earned my M.A. at Toronto with a focus on Canadian Studies. I spent the next five years after my M.A. teaching Canadian Studies in the Province of Ontario, Canada. In the process, I have created long-lasting friendships with Canadians, and we still share insights and best practices. A key forum for this sharing has been our Canadian Research Center blog. The insights which follow come from the blog in order to share our creative comparisons with you as useful benchmarks, guides to best practices, also.

Paul Rux, Ph.D. (Wisconsin-Madison), M.A. (Toronto)

Topic 1: Canadian Concern about Virulent American Nationalism from Terrorism

Walter, thank you for taking time to share your perspectives.   Sadly, we have the 9/11 catastrophe that continues to haunt folks here. Twice as many Americans died on 9/11 than at Pearl Harbor in 1941. So, it is reasonable to know who is here. Canada has done a good job, to date, except for the recent killing at the tomb of the unknowns in Ottawa, and the FLQ crisis of 1971, in keeping track of potential terrorism. My view is, they are over here, because we are over there. I grew up in a family with classic American Isolationist roots. We will do business with you, but we want no foreign entanglements as George Washington advised in his now-forgotten Farewell Address. Our oil wars in Afghanistan and Iraq, plus the Zionist lobby here, have embroiled us in the affairs of others, when there is oil in Alberta.

What we are seeing is a return to "tribalism" and end of the Enlightenment's hope for a cosmopolitan world. I just finished reading Robert Kagan's book *The Return of History and the End of Dreams*, published in 2009, in which Kagan, who works for the Carnegie Endowment for Peace, argues this point. I think it is safe to say that recent events in Europe align with Kagan's prediction, futuristic forecasting. Of course, the mass media engages in drama to sell advertising, and this, in turn, leads to demagoguery, as you observe. I want to be fair, but fear, fear of terrorism, can, and, sadly, is undermining fair, because terrorism is real and creates real fear, its goal. There, those are my thoughts. Hopefully the USA will return to its Isolationist roots and stop sowing the seeds of our own destruction. Take care, and thank you for your honest sharing, again. Paul

Posted by Paul Rux, Ph.D. at 5:48 P

Topic 2: Canada - National Election - October 2015 - Canadian Viewpoint

Hi Paul,
If the "new conservatives" inspired by Rove and American wedge issue politics are out of power, we the people will win. If whoever forms the new government can start to address the country as a whole rather than special interest groups, we will be on a better course.

Maybe Canadians have become more engaged through the transparent lies they have been fed in this campaign, but I fear that as usual the majority of Canadian follow American 'news' more than Canadian and as a result know more about Trump and are victims of American fear-mongering and militaristic attitudes.

My vote was easy since there is a strong local candidate whom I know well and respect both in terms of ability and character.

Our political system does need an overhaul. The PMO has evolved into a centralized seat of power that has no real checks if there is a majority in the House. Traditions of Parliament are ignored- omnibus bills like in the USA, the PM acting like a president rather than allowing the G.-G to perform the functions of a head of state. The Senate has become a reward system for party hacks rather than a chamber of 'sober' second thought, the kind of thinking we need desperately.

We, like the rest of western civilization (Gandhi's quip applies: western civilization, a good idea, if had ever been tried) have lost our way and become stupid since we now actually behave as though it's only about the economy, stupid."

If you add in the atavistic tendencies of the religious right we have a recipe for global disaster.

Globally there are tectonic shifts occurring that we cannot control- the rise and decline of nations, depletion of resources...........and few political leaders understand them and fewer can communicate them given our 10 second attention spans.

I'm hoping that our election has scrabbled the pieces enough so that we can start creating a new message for our society. What that will be and how it will work its way into action, I can only guess. I'm hoping we look at ourselves honestly and redress some of the real harm we have done in our past and build on the human and natural wealth we have already built.

Cheers,
walter

Topic 3: The Old School Tie in Canada

Stephanie, I have seen the house system work big time at Upper Canada College, Toronto, Canada. It is the Eaton/Harrow/Ruby elite high school for boys in Canada. It has "houses." This gives each student a special identity and provides the basis for internal competition in sports, academics, and social events. However, all "houses" focus on overall excellence in all aspects of student life. The "houses" help to remove isolation, build friendships among students, and instill a sense of intramural pride and competition that drives overall excellence. I taught at nearby St. Andrew's College, an elite school in the model of Upper Canada College. We were rivals in the same prep school league. At St. Andrew's, which immigrants from Scotland founded, we did not have "houses." We had "clans." The purpose of the "clans" at St. Andrew's was the same as the "houses" at Upper Canada College. At St. Andrew's each clan had ties with the tartan of the actual clan in Scotland on it to wear when they competed in intra-mural events. In the end, however, they all wore the St. Andrew's school tie with pride; your humble servant has his St. Andrew's tie to this very day too! Dr. Rux

Topic 4: Videos and Confederation of the Great Lakes

Nicholas, this is thoughtful, thorough, and provides valuable insights. One, the visual culture trend jumps out at your humble servant as he goes through various discount, thrift, retail stores here in Florida over the past three months. What he sees is lots of romance paperbacks; serious factual books are disappearing. The same is happening in large retail giants like Wal-Mart. The video disc section is twice as large as the print section, which includes magazines like *Guns and Ammo*. Yesterday, this writer visited the historical museum in Cedar Key, Florida. The volunteer at the desk, a retired M.D. from New York, told me that not one book store exists in Levy County. The last one was across the street from the museum, which a retired M.D. from Michigan opened and ran. He and I became friends over the years; it was one of my favorite stops there. His wife got sick, and they had to return north. The book store is now empty, up for rent. You get the idea.

Two, your discussion of economic domains reminds me of the Canadian consul general from Chicago who a year ago came to speak at a luncheon in the Madison Club, Madison, Wisconsin. He said, given the population, production, water transportation the Provinces of Canada and the State of America on the Great Lakes could easily create a Federation, the Federation of the Great Lakes he called it! It would not need the rest of the areas like Kentucky, South Dakota, Manitoba, etc. to become prosperous. It would trade with them, but it would not provide corporate and social welfare for them! This is economic domain big time; yes, it was suggested during the US Civil War. Northerners who opposed fighting Southern planters for Wall Street banks suggested a Northwest Confederation, similar to the Great Lakes proposal. They said what went on in Dixie was none of their concern; they could use the Great Lakes to make a living without cotton! If Wall Street and Washington are not careful, such projects could easily emerge. They would rely on economic domains, not political boundaries, as their engines. If this country experiences institutional failure, which it could do yet, look for such economic domains springing into autonomous life and shedding the parasites on them. Thanks for listening. Dr. Rux

Topic 5: Winning and Losing in Wiarton, Ontario, Canada

Walter, wow, wow, wow! I love your reflections. Please keep them coming. I also concur with your analysis in the email below 100%. Pollster John Zogby in 2008 detected a trend in the U.S. He called it "authentic." You state this here. People, he estimates it at 48% then, are moving toward the value of "authenticity." They are tired of fakes, phonies, and frauds lying to them, exploiting them, and destroying them. Zogby argues Americans have two traditions. One is commercial; the other is conscience. New England has its roots in Puritan conscience, not commerce, which came later. Walden Pond is a symbol of this authenticity, and Zogby says Americans, and Canadians too, as North Americans, are moving more and more toward their versions of Walden Pond. They are willing to work for less if they can have time for themselves and those whom they love, their neighbors, communities. You document this superbly in your description of the musical event in Barrie, Ontario, Canada. There is hope in this. One of the best experiences of my life was the four years in Wiarton, Ontario, Canada. I did not know it at the time, but my time there was one of the few in my lifetime where I felt a sense of community, which is absolutely basic to mental, social health. At the time, I thought it was exile; as the Chinese say, who is winning and losing depends on when you ask the question. Now, maturity has framed those years as one of the greatest learning, living experiences of my life. Dear friend, we see the world the same way. It is comforting to know that you value what I do, see what I do, and hope for what I do. Please consider collecting your poetry, essays into some book format. It could be paperback. It could be self-published. Make it your heritage to those seeking authentic. God bless, Paul

Topic 6: Promises in Canada to Keep Before I Sleep

Gary, this is terrific! Your use of wild card and historical analyses are stunning. Your first article in particular grabbed the attention of this writer. Here is why. I earned my M.A. at the University of Toronto; I studied with John S. Moir, the greatest church historian ever in Canada. Sadly, he died in 2012. When I last saw him, he took me alone into his story at his home. He said, "Do a study of the future of religion in Canada. Immigration is going to change this country forever, and religious trends will change with it." I honor Prof. Moir as my role model, hero; I am starting to take steps toward funding to do this. Your article has simply fired up my resolution to honor my promise to Prof. Moir and write and publish a study in his honor. Thank you Gary for your "push" here.   When you wrote your analysis you had no way of knowing its special impact on your humble servant here. Thank you. Thank you. Dr. Paul Rux

Topic 7: Knowledge Access in Canada - and Beyond

Thanks Paul,

Seldom do I agree as much as with this trends summary. Already made some adjustments in my portfolio in anticipation.   I'm not confident our gurus can prevent a period of stagflation and that will be really painful.

The one I question most is online education. It is the only platform that makes sense for everyday training, but I think that the really good stuff will be for those with $$$$$$$$$$$ sort of like insider trading. Corporations and governments control data the way the church used to. The noose is tightening rather than easing in Canada. Knowledge is now a traded commodity which is bad for humanity. What is free is mostly on the level gossip, uninformed opinion, outdated and junk science, and titillation that pas for curiosity.
A trend that I would add is getting off the grid and small is finally recognized as beautiful. The only mid to long term solution in the 'developed' world is to pull back on economic expectations and consumer culture- back to 1940s-50s level of consumption and knowing how to do things for ourselves. Any visit to a supermarket reveals how packaged life is. That's not sustainable and not good.

Stormy outside.

Cheers,
Walter

Topic 8: J.S. Moir, Ph.D., University of Toronto, Professional Example

Your humble servant here admires your determination, grit as doctoral students to hang on and hang in with your studies despite challenges in your personal lives, e.g. health issues. Your consistent first-class work is even more impressive when you share some of the background to your lives with your humble servant here. Thank you for this sharing. It honors, continues a tradition that began full-force in my life when I had such a sharing relationships with the late Prof. J.S. Moir at the University of Toronto, where I was a Graduate Fellow for a M.A. Yes, our work is professional; it is also personal. This does not mean "personality psycho-babble stuff." It means genuine sharing, rapport between student, teacher. Right now I am studying Confucius; he emphasizes the value of the master-student (teacher-student) relationship as one of the great relationships that we humans can experience. You are going to have such relationships with your own students as professors after your doctoral degrees. Continue the tradition. Dr. Rux

Topic 9: Win and Compete to Educate

Jeanine, wow, thank you for sharing this.   Folks like your humble servant here suspect such things; you offer proof. What changes things is the lack of money. Education does not need more money - this does not mean cutting pay for teachers. It needs less funding so it must asking the first question: In what business are we? In addition, a country that knows how to win wars and compete economically will know how to educate its youth. Sadly, America is losing the capacity to win and compete for now. You may find the attached "speech" for my Rotary (Madison, WI, West) Club on Thursday of this week of interest, for it is one way of expressing what is missing. Thank you for your sharing. Dr. Rux (This applies equally to Canada.) The "win and compete" insight in fact comes from the late *Toronto Globe and Mail* columnist Richard J. Needham, a favorite of this writer.)

Topic 10: Rights without duties in Canada

Hi Paul,
It's starting to sound like Italian politics. With most public institutions in disrepute anything can happen. Credibility has been shifted to the noise makers. Whatever happened to enlightened despotism like in the 18th C?

Topic 10: Rights without duties in Canada

I suspect that our countries and global structures are simply too big to regulate and even more difficult for most people to understand. The alternative is to think local and act locally, not think global and act locally as the idealists suggest. The word revolution keeps cropping up in many contexts. Let's keep our eye on where revolution is happening and see if we could face that set of circumstances. I'm trying my best to stay sane. I think I may revive the Rhinoceros Party which had one item in its platform: if elected an MP would resign. In my riding back in the 70s we generated some buzz and garnered 5% of the vote.

I sometimes reflect back on a discussion I started with my students a decade or so ago about citizenship in the broad context of values and ethics. My question to them was, "do you think you owe anything to your society/". They were silent. It became apparent that the vast majority had no sense of obligation tcwards their country if what was meant by that was service to our society, as in voluntary work for minimal pay for months or even years. They saw the benefits of society as their right with no apparent obligations beyond waving a flag and cheerleading. I'm proud to be Canadian but don't ask me to actually do anything for my country!
I have not been able to sort this out satisfactorily because kids still are idealistic and want to make things better. The analogy that I find useful is that of the 'fabric' of society. Fabric is made from many strands, often in many colors and patterns. The quality of the strands and the quality of the weaving are paramount if the fabric is going to function well. If the weave is too loose it weakens even if the strands are strong. If the weave is too strong for the strands, it tears. So we can have colorful fabric in our society but when we actually have to use it, it needs to be well-made. There are many torn strands in society throughout the world and the winds of change are blowing through the holes. We are desperately trying to patch a worn out fabric.

Ventura and Stern I suspect, know how to tear things apart but probably not how to weave things together,

Walter

PS. My daughter-in-law commented yesterday how quickly I can go from the practical to the theoretical on any topic. I've done it again, it seems.

Topic 11: Will Canada follow USA union busting trend?

Shaun, unfortunately, I do not know offhand of any seminal works about this topic. It is a fascinating one, for the current governor of Wisconsin broke the public service unions, which includes state tech/junior colleges. We have daily protests, literally daily, five days a week, in our state capital because of this. The union members and friends conduct a sing-along under the dome in the state capitol at noon. It has resulted in arrests and ongoing "bad blood." The governor did not announce during the election his union-busting agenda; it came as a total surprise! As I write this, I do not know how many other states in fact have taken this route. Yes, your question about union impact on operations and learning outcomes is timely, crucial. It may be a good time to explore how widespread union-busting is right now in education. How has union busting helped or hurt? Meanwhile, as you observe, how has the union presence helped or hurt outcomes, operations where unions are still legal? This is a great issue. Lack of unions means lack of tenure, job security. More and more we are becoming Daniel Pink's classic *Free Agent Nation*. Yes, as an administrator, you may face challenges over unions, busting them, keeping them. FYI Your humble servant has been a member of public teacher unions in both Ontario, Canada and Illinois, USA. In fact, he went on strike in Ontario. He is a friend of unions because of the due process pressure they exert on management. Yet, he operates as a "free agent" as he types this. This is a very good issue to pursue. It is not going away soon. Dr. Rux

Topic 12: Future of Natural Resources

Walter, thank you for confirming my suspicions of the downside of this.   Here, the fracking would occur on the banks of the Wisconsin River, and the danger of its contamination looms. It is crazy. As Freud observed, humans have two subconscious drives - Eros, to live, and Thanatos, to die. It is always a race between the two; of late, it seems Thanatos is gaining on Eros. Thanks for your update. Yes, the Great Lakes are a vital resource. Americans and Canadians too, live in an illusion of endless natural resources. There are, however, limits (conservative word, concept there); we are approaching them. In our Anglo-Saxon heritage the story of Robin Hood sums up the popular culture. It goes like this. Robin lives in the forest preserve, the king's forest; of course, anything associated with the king is bad. Hence, conservation, reservation of natural resources by the king, aka the state, is bad. You get the drift. Thanks for listening. I am grateful to be able to share. Paul

Topic 13: Elora calling

Walter, in 2013 Jane and I need to get out butts over to Ontario so we can visit with you and D-K in person, live, face to face. It's been too long. Thank you for keeping in touch, sharing your wisdom, and your friendship. You are the best. Meanwhile, the Republic teeters along. Jane and I will vote for Obama and the rest of the Democrats. We believe in fairness; the Wall Street gangsters control even more of the Republicans than they do of the Democrats. Besides, we need our Social Security and Medicare now. People here are somber. You see few bumper stickers, yard signs, buttons, etc. They know the "wheels are coming off the wagon" and the gangsters on Wall Street and their stooges in Washington - despite the horrific economic damage here, which is still mounting. The American people overall are good people when they remain true to their historical values. I make no apology for the "old time religion," for it brought me to Canada. The Pilgrims, New Englanders believed in the sanctity of "Conscience"; it became my heritage too. Canada today is where America was in the 1950's. It is a sane, balanced place yet; people there still have a sense of optimism that is sadly missing here. The best part is Canada remains a fabulous reminder of what once was here and could be here again! Thank you for the comparison. I sorely miss the Great Dominion to our North. It preserves American "know-how" without the violence. I guess at heart I remain an old Loyalist, "old school," Conservative, in the true sense of the word, concept, cf. Edmund Burke, one of my heroes. Anyway, Elora, Ontario keeps calling me now. My old friends in Wiarton have been dying out; thankfully, Elora has emerged to start a new cycle for me. I love Old Ontario, its ways. God willing, I will establish ongoing connections with it; it is not far from Barrie!

Topic 14: Future of Religion in Canada

Marta, at the conference, I met a young Canadian woman who immigrated to Canada from the Middle East. She lives in Windsor, Ontario, and has a MBA from the University of Edinburgh in Scotland. She is a wonderful person. I plan to explore how she and I can co-author a book on the future of religion in Canada. I studied at the U of Toronto with the greatest historian of religion in Canada, ever, John S. Moir as part of my M.A. from there. He died last year. When I last saw him he asked me to do this study for him. Out of loyalty I plan to do it. Right now, I want to use the mind mapping approach to conduct depth interviews with expert people. Having a devout Muslim woman on the team would enhance the objectivity and credibility of the study. Our 1.5 hour session at the Chicago World Future Society Conference 2013 came away with this trend. As the economy worsens, which it will in this country for sure, people more and more will turn to religion for solace, comfort.

Topic 14: Future of Religion in Canada

They will give up on the false gods of money, politics, materialism and return to what is "authentic." If however the USA embarks on a war against Iran we can also expect the emergence of fundamentalism and hostility between Christians and Muslims. In fact, one of the mind maps at the conference centered on War with Iran in 2018! Is this probable? Is it possible? It most surely, probability there, would lead to fundamentalist backlashes in both Christian and Muslim communities, sadly.

There, you have a concise summary of what emerged at the conference. I hope we have sense enough to stop wars and seek common ground on core values, since both Muslims and Christians - and Jews - share the Old Testament in common. The Prophet called these three religions "People of the Book" and called for Muslims to treat the "People of the Book" with exceptional kindness, concern, and "family" - like love. It is amazing how oil politics distorts and ignores core teachings.

Topic 15: Brazil and Canada and USA

Marta, the panel on the future of Latin America was stunning at the WFS conference in Chicago over the weekend. At the workshop was a past President (three times elected) of the Dominican Republic! I had an exciting visit with him. Here is an example of what the panel presented. Brazil purchases more from the USA right now than all of Europe combined! And we are busy jabbering about Europe in our mass media with hardly a word about Brazil!

Topic 16: Declining Value of American Tourists in Canada

Hi Paul,

Unfortunately the wealth gap can keep growing if seen on a global scale. The empires have always used colonies to subsidize internal standards of living and it is only when the empires decline that the internal gaps in wealth become troubling. In 1965 America GIs could live off base in Germany and drive a Porsche if they wished. By the 1980s they could only afford to live on base and shop at the PX as Europeans caught up to the American Empire. American tourists used to dominate the world market. Having just returned from Europe it is striking that I met not one American but lots of Asians. In Canada American visitors are no longer a priority because they spend a fraction- about 1/3 of what Asian visitors spend. Americans are better off than in 1950 but their relative position in the world has changed and that puts the focus on internal gaps. Psychologically this is a well established phenomenon: a relatively lower wage hurts far more than a nominally lower wage as long as you make more than the next guy.

Topic 16: Declining Value of American Tourists in Canada

The empire has the costs of maintaining the structure for elite who are unwilling to pay for it.

The myths of "free enterprise" - there have never been such a condition- perpetuate a Utopian dream of easy money for everyone. Globalization has undermined the nation state to a point where the laws are written by corporations who have no national loyalty. They are the new empires and the citizens of countries are patsies to these corporate behemoths- most agricultural subsidies go to large corporations (read ethanol), most science subsidies go to large corporations, even private prisons are subsidized (a good private prison is where the "customers" keep coming back.
Most egregiously, the military are run for the benefit of corporations -read Haliburton- with $200 hammers and a propaganda machine that keeps people in terror while more people are committing suicide each year for various reasons despite almost no visible terrorist threat.

We no longer talk of citizens, but rather taxpayers and our focus is on spending (making a living) rather than making a life worth living. Our language has been co-opted by the true believers (Hoffer) in money and the message is broadcast through advertising which is the air we breathe well beyond anything Orwell presented in 1984, Stalin was able to achieve through brutality and murder by the millions, or Goebbels with the Nazis. Obesity, drug addiction, fanatic sports aimless "malling" are all symptoms of this social malaise. Remember 'the lonely crowd'?

The correction is happening. We will eventually need to find a way to help people live lives, build communities and societies rather than give them "freedom' to flail about in a world governed by forces they can't even imagine let alone control.

This isn't an American, but rather a western challenge. With 25% educated youth unemployed in most of the West there is great potential for social unrest like in the 30s. The 'Freeters' in Japan are a cautionary tale.

Posted by Paul Rux, Ph.D. at 8:28 PM

Topic 17: Toronto points to the future.

Jason, look for educational technology, e.g. simulations, which are cheap and self-paced to more and more displace teachers, professors. Digital technology has the capacity now to "automate" learning and relegate teachers to the role of facilitators more and more. Teaching is what somebody does to us. Learning is what we do for ourselves; what we do for ourselves in the final analysis has more lasting impact. Call it discovery learning if you need a theory, name for it. The teacher unions here in Wisconsin are already worrying about this looming trend; higher education will also embrace the trend. We are in short looking at "teacherless" education, one of the core workshops at the 2012 World Future Society in Toronto, which your humble servant here had the good fortune to attend. 2013 is in Chicago! Closer.

Topic 18: Oxford Style - in Canada

Ronda, think of our course this way. It is "Oxford style." At Oxford University, students get a tutor. They meet with their tutors one-to-one weekly. The tutor assigns reading; the student does the reading. Then, both student and tutor meet the following week to discuss the readings. The tutor, of course, is a world-class expert who likely has done all of the reading on the topics that libraries can provide! I had the great honor of engaging in such a learning experience at the University of Toronto for one entire academic year! Once weekly, I met one-to-one with Prof. John S. Moir, who passed away last year, ouch. He gave me reading assignments. Go to the library and read about this and that topic. Then, I would come back a week later to discuss what I had discovered and read on the subject with him! The bond between us became powerful, personal, and highly professional. We remained in contact after I earned my M.A. from Toronto under his guidance. This included periodic visits with him and his wife at their home in Brantford, Ontario. I told him when we last visited, two years ago, that he remains my hero; I want to be to my students what he was to me. There, we are going to do our course "Oxford style," although it will be only for eight weeks, not an academic year of nine months. Sadly, the factory model of learning has marginalized this one-to-one learning style, method. Yet, when we experience it, we never forget it. We can have this "Oxford style" experience.

Topic 19: Lean Learning

Yes, education is a business; as our economy tanks and budgets crash with it, more and more you will see a business ROI - return on investment - approach to education replace the trendy psycho-babble that now runs it. Watch for application of such techniques as "lean manufacturing" - doing more with less - to education. The days of more are over. Educators are going to "hit the wall" - get a reality check - soon because of this.

Topic 20: Can Canada avoid trends in American education?

Dave, thank you for this.   What's missing is the collapsing standards overall as the educational dinosaurs scramble to enroll bodies - real and fake - to get cash flow at any cost. Except for hardcore subjects like medicine, the M.D. hopefully will not get watered down, and fields like no-nonsense engineering; the other subject areas, the "soft sciences" and the humanities will suffer from Gresham's Law - "bad money drives out good money."

Topic 20: Can Canada avoid trends in American education?

Degrees will have little or no meaning or value in these fields, unless they come from very elite, tough standards, no-nonsense college or universities. As one of my UW-Madison professors put it in our course on ethics of higher education, "The colleges and universities that keep high, high standards will always be in demand, for there will always be people with money to buy the best." Also, he observed, to create such high standards you could not let the business office call the shots. You had to let high academic values, standards set the agenda; the money would follow. Instead we have the reverse in more and more cases. Making money in the short run regardless of standards will blow up the organizations peddling valueless degrees. The one with hard, tough, steely academic standards will in fact survive and make money. As A.J. Nock observed, "Americans have a gift for turning everything into a racket." In this case, so-called higher education has become a racket. In the end, however, people will not pay for fake degrees, and those who are serious and can benefit from learning will go to those places that have maintained good-and-hard standards. There, you have your humble servant's studied opinion. Paul

Topic 21: Look South Not North

Sonia, this is thoughtful. To it, let me add this. Ralph Peters, one of the leading military strategists in our country, in his latest books, *New Glory*, argues that America's future is to the South, Latin America, not Europe or the Middle East, or Asia, any longer. Latin America has the resources, markets, and human resources we need to keep our economy moving and support our aging population. Therefore the issue of knowing Spanish will become increasingly important in America, and for incoming Hispanics to America knowing English will be crucial also. We are moving into a new era of hope if we refocus South. Your interest in promoting ESL is on trend, and, yes, much needed.

Topic 22: How similar are trends in Canada to trends in USA?

I have no respect for the government anymore'
Welcome to The Michael Savage Newsletter, your daily insider report on all things "Savage."
In today's issue: It just so happened that Michael Savage's Tuesday night show coincided with President Obama's State of the Union address.

"You can listen to this Politbureau speech on other radio stations across America if you want to," Savage told his audience, adding, "All I see is a bunch of grafters slapping each other on the back."

"Watching the prelude to the State of the Union speech, I feel like I'm looking at the Ukrainian parliament," said a disgusted Dr. Savage, adding:

The only difference is, they'd be punching each other out. At least we the people would get some entertainment out of that.
All I see is a bunch of grifters slapping each other on the back. You just know they're cutting deals in the back room.
I don't even feel it's my country anymore.
I have no faith in them. I have no respect for this anymore.
And I'm not going to sit and watch this clown giving another speech calling for higher taxes and more regulation, and listen to the stooges on the Democrat side clap like a bunch of seals.
That's all Obama's talking about: tax and spend. Soft Marxism and hard crony capitalism.
Tax the people. Control the people from cradle to grave, and then reward your crony capitalist friends by not taxing them, or giving them sweetheart contracts and grants.
Do you really feel that you live in a representative democracy?

Topic 23: Fair Canada and Unfair USA

Walter, here are some thoughts on Obama's impressive speech. He is clearly an accomplished speaker, big time.

The key word, concept is fair. A Canadian from Burlington, Ontario, who attends Rotary here with me, said in conversation with me that in simplest terms the difference between Canada and the USA is fairness.

Canada practices fairness. I have lived it.

For example, nobody goes bankrupt in Canada because of medical bills. They do here. Last month, we were in a discount store, and Jane engaged the young woman behind the checkout register in short conversation. The clerk was working two minimum-wage jobs to pay off $8,000 in medical bills! This does not happen in Canada. The USA is not fair. Greed rules supreme here now.

Topic 23: Fair Canada and Unfair USA

The two parts of his speech, brief, but scary, that caught my attention big time were his backing of Israel, in effect, against Iran. The entire chamber roared approval - for the next war. Obama's bringing Hagel into the cabinet as secretary of defense is part of the run-up, "bipartisan" support for the next war in the Middle East. North Korea is a "loose cannon" too, and it could get bloody.

As my late UT professor, J.S. Moir observed, Canada in effect is 30 million Democrats. You repeat his observation too.

Often, what is not said is as important as what is said. For instance, there was no mention of recovering the loot stolen from the American people by the bloodsucking vampires on Wall Street. Big Money owns Washington, DC here. More and more what occurs there has no connection to the "little people" outside the "Beltway." Fakes, phonies and frauds populate D.C.

Yes, Obama put on a good show. He got it right about starvation wages. For instance, here in Citrus County, Florida, the average annual wage is, yes, $17,000. A husband and wife might buy a used trailer house on such pittance; they do. When we go to Wal-Mart here we see lots of "rough" people, the $17,000/year persons living in the shadows here. It is disgusting. It is not fair.
We see good, honest people here each and every day. The American people are good people; we are an abused people. It is not fair that the people, who do the work, obey the laws, pay the taxes, and, yes, fight the wars, get ripped off left and right here. My concern is another war in the Middle East will "pull down the house" on them, us. At some point, they are going to get mad.

God bless. Take care. Paul

Topic 24: Keep the Gun Crazies out of Canada

Walter, thank you for this thoughtful, as always, reply. I concur with all of it.

I do not own any guns; I do not want to own any guns. As you point out, this gun stuff is toxic to tourism. The other more potent threat, however, is the recruiting of former Special Forces alumni into private mercenary groups like Blackwater.

They are the highly-armed, disciplined, experienced shock troops, or Praetorian Guards, to support the corporate power structure if and when push comes to shoves. Compared with Blackwater, the NRA is amateurs, and if the NRA gets in the way, Blackwater will crush them. It is disgusting; more and more we are reluctant to venture into public places, e.g. movie houses. Online education will get a boost from this spreading terrorism, call it what it is; online shopping, too, will benefit from this growing fear of public places because of the gun nuts out there. It has reached the point that one of my online students, a doctoral student, in Texas, tells me teachers there now lock their classroom doors out of fear! Thank God you live where you do; do not let the rot, cancer of gun mania poison Canada. This includes taking a swift severe line with the mutants who shoot up places like Toronto. Stop it now, good and hard. It is bed time now. Paul

Topic 25: Federation of the Great Lakes

Marshall, this is first-class, thoughtful, thorough, and of obvious practical value. Your humble servant here more and more embraces the concept of "economic domains" instead of political boundaries. For instance, Dubuque, Iowa, on the Mississippi River forms a natural tri-state economic domain with SW Wisconsin and NW Illinois. Folks there are starting to realize this and act on it. Great! What happens in Madison, WI, Springfield, IL, and Des Moines, IA - except for taxing and regulations - has little if anything to do with the economic health of this tri-state interface. Yes, economic domains, not political boundaries are the future engines. The consul general of Canada from Chicago told an audience last year, where this writer was in attendance, that the Great Lakes states, Ontario and Quebec could easily form an economic domain without the baggage of the rest of the political structures to east, west, and south. He said such an economic domain would create the 7th largest economy in the world - and 14th largest population concentration! We are, yes, edging toward understanding and applying the insights of "economic domains" in the future.

Topic 26: Can Canada escape American educational trends?

The trend in higher education, so-called, is toward low-paid "educational workers" here. It is the factory model, pure and simple. This is why I am gravitating toward training and development, for at least it is still honest about what it offers, how it offers it, and aligns with the emerging workforce needs. Yes, you are right. It is destroying the traditional university model.

A few elite places will survive, but most of the others are degree
mills, and if they are not, they are on their ways to becoming
them. In Wisconsin, the state cut the state university system budgets
by 40%. They are running around like "chicken little" with the "sky
falling on them." The powerhouse places like Madison, of course, have
the R&D base to secure grants and an alumni network to secure $150
million yearly in donations. The others are treading water for dear
life. Yes, the rules are changing. Right now, we are, if we are
honest, not sure what the new ones are. For instance, I have proposed
a workshop for the 2013 Chicago conference of the World Future Society
on the "Death of Teamwork." Enter Harry Pink's *Free Agent
Nation*. More and more people are no around long enough to establish
teamwork.

Topic 27: Branch Plant Economy in Canada

This writer first learned about the toxins of branch plant economies when he lived
and worked in Canada for eight years. It was at the heart of the debate about
Canada's future.

Barbara, this is a first-class analysis of the social impacts of a business. Recently, I
attended a meeting with the director of the Wisconsin Technology Council, which
seeks to bring jobs to the state. Note the word bring. Instead of growing new
businesses here his idea is to get big companies to open branch plants here. However,
since the branch plant's owners do not live here, they care little if anything for how
operations impact the community, as long as it makes money for them. In short,
absent owners have no loyalties to the branch plant communities. This is what passes
for economic development in this state.

Topic 28: Bullying of Teachers in Ontario

The following message went to an American online doctoral student of educational
administration. However, friends in Ontario, Canada tell this writer that such bullying
is standard practice there too.

Ylonda, this is first-rate, and it earns full credit. Here is something for you to
consider. In the view of this writer, one of the key reasons students arrive under-
prepared, or not prepared at all, is bullying of teachers by students. Yes, our systems
allow students to bully teachers by not backing teachers to set standards for
academics and behaviors.

Teachers ought to have total control over who is in their classrooms and on what terms persons are in their classrooms, not principals or guidance counselors. This would restore dignity to teaching as a profession with professional autonomy and respect. Right now, overall, they are treated like cogs in a machine. The result is student bullying of teachers for the system in effect permits, encourages it. Until teachers can discipline, magic word there, discipline, students again we can expect standards to continue to crumble. Perhaps your research ought to explore bullying of teachers. What do you think?

Topic 29: Superior Educational Standards in Ontario, Canada

Brian, my model is Ontario, Canada. When I studied, worked there you had to have a minimum of five years in the classroom before you could apply to take the principal's course. You also had to be a classroom teacher in your subject field before you could apply to take the advanced training to become a department chair. And you had to serve as a department chair before you could apply to be a principal. I completed the department chair training in social studies; I never served as a chair. Yes, as the old West Point saying goes, "To give an order, you must first learn how to take an order." This applies to education too.

Topic 30: Canadian Trends Point toward USA War against Iran

Canada has closed its embassy in Iran and brought its entire Foreign Service folks home. This is a signal that it is putting distance between itself and what is about to happen when the USA attacks Iran. A bank manager friend of mine tonight told me that one of his clerks has a son in our military who has gone back to that part of the world again. Before leaving he told her that plans are underway to go to war with Iran. This coincides with the closing of the Canadian embassy. Likely the gangsters in Washington will wait until after the holidays to launch. It would be bad PR to ruin the coming holiday season. As my late sainted uncle liked to say, "Same tune, second verse." God bless. Paul

Topic 31: "Red Tories" the "One Nation" Canadian Conservative Tradition

John, thank you for the superb definition of "One Nation" Conservatives. This describes your humble servant here perfectly. A year or two ago, you and I spoke briefly about the "red Tory" - fair play for all - tradition in British, and Canadian, politics. I learned about it when I lived and studied in Ontario, Canada for eight years. You caught me by surprise when in our short visit you also knew about it too!

Otto von Bismarck would be a "One Nation" Conservative too. Classic conservative thought as you know views society as organic, similar to the human body, in which all the parts must be healthy for the body to be healthy. What in fact masquerades as Conservative thought here too often, far too often, in fact, is classic 18-19th-century Liberalism, in which the Individual can divorce from society and not care about the health of the whole. This is the rationale, if you need one, for the destructive greed at work in our American "body politic" sadly for too many years now. In short, the Canadian or British "Red Tory" or the "One Nation" Conservat've believes in fairness for all - without having to sacrifice the traditional values and heritage that have stood the tests of time. Thank you for helping your humble servant here to see more clearly the sad impasse which we have reached in our country. Keep up your good work. Paul

Topic 32: Thanatos Sadly Is Alive and Well in Canada Too

Carl, Freud observed humans have two subconscious drives. One is Eros (source of word erotic), the drive to live. The second is Thanatos, a drive to die, a subconscious death wish. Freud observed that reason (ego) and social tradition (super ego) around us serve as a check on Thanatos, when reason (ego) and social tradition (super ego) work well. When reason and tradition weaken, look for self-destructive behaviors. For example, alcoholics and drug addicts, in effect, have a death wish for they defy logic and social wisdom accumulated by the human race over centuries. It is amazing to observe the death wish in our own society, for more and more it acts in irrational ways and in defiance of human wisdom accumulated over centuries of hard experience. Pick your examples of such death-wish behaviors.

Topic 33: Happy in Canada

Hi Paul,

 Here's something to make you smile. I often think we are complainers and the Danes I've known have been crusty but perhaps it says something about not trying to be #1 or even 2 or #3.

Happy? You Must Be From Canada

The Guelph Mercury, September 26, 2012
If you're happy and you know it, a new report suggests you might be from Canada.

The Centre for the Study of Living Standards says more than 90 per cent of Canadians surveyed report they are either satisfied or very satisfied with their lives. The centre tracked numbers collected by Statistics Canada in its community health survey between 2003 and 2011.

Canadians have stayed happy through that entire period, with 91 per cent reporting life satisfaction in 2003 and 92 per cent saying so last year.

The scores were enough to officially rank Canada as among the happiest countries in the world.

The centre says a Gallup world poll taken in February 2012 rated Canada as the second most satisfied nation, ranked only behind Denmark.

Centre executive director Andrew Sharpe said the numbers tell a compelling story about the standard of living most Canadians enjoy.

"We do have high levels of income. We have weathered the financial crisis better than other countries of the world," Sharpe said in a telephone interview. "We do have a good health system. We complain about it, but at least there's full coverage of all Canadians . . . We do have a lot of advantages as a country."

The StatsCan data - compiled in biennial surveys between 2003 and 2007 and in annual surveys from 2008 onward - asked Canadians to rate their own levels of personal satisfaction on a scale of 0 to 10.

Those who assigned themselves a score of 6 or above were considered to be pleased with their lives as a whole.

The numbers have remained relatively static in most cases, but Sharpe said some age-related trends have begun to emerge in the most recent figures.

More of Canada's young people are reporting feeling contented, while the country's senior citizens are expressing more reservations about their lot in life, he said, adding the gap between the two age groups has widened considerably over the past several years.

About 94 per cent of Canadians between 12 and 19 years of age reported feeling satisfied in 2003 compared to 92 per cent of those over 65.

By 2001, the number of satisfied seniors had fallen to 89 per cent while youth happiness scores had shot up to 97 per cent.

Sharpe attributed some of the change to the economic turmoil that has roiled the job market and depleted savings for those nearing retirement, leaving the country's youngest residents comparatively unscathed.

The data, however, suggests there may be other factors at work causing seniors to feel less positive as they age.

Sharpe said the stats show the need for policy-makers to analyze issues impacting seniors, since current approaches appear to be coming up short.

The trend among Canada's aging demographic illustrate why it's important to track happiness alongside gross domestic product and other more traditional indicators of well-being, he said.

"I think the goal should be to improve happiness. It sounds trite, but what's it all about? It's about the life satisfaction of Canadians," Sharpe said.

Satisfaction levels also differed by region, according to the centre's analysis.

Average scores taken over the eight-year period suggest residents of Nova Scotia, Quebec and Newfoundland and Labrador were most likely to be happy with their lives. Satisfaction scores were lowest in British Columbia, Ontario and Nunavut.

The StatsCan data that formed the basis of the centre's report was gathered from 65,000 people nationwide but excluded some of the populations most likely to report dissatisfaction with their lives.

The Canadian Community Health Survey does not collect data from people living on aboriginal reserves, full-time members of the Canadian Forces or those currently in institutions.

Sharpe acknowledged data from those excluded demographics could lower scores, adding even the current high numbers should sound a cautionary note.

"I don't want to go to complacency. 'Oh, aren't we great,' therefore there are no problems in Canada. That's not where this is going," he said. "We can do better."

Topic 34: 2012 Differences between USA and Canada

Hi,

This was an opinion piece in the *Toronto Star* and I have to agree that I am also puzzled by the election in the USA.

I also think that the piece in the NY Times on American exceptionalism gets at a crucial point that America will have to come to grips with: God is not on America's side and never was. If you are a Christian he is on the side of the righteous, but hardly behind groups. Is god a chauvinist?

"Americans have one of the lowest participation rates in elections — only about 50 per cent in the presidential race. Yet they are very much engaged in politics. They do tune into their leaders' televised debates — 68 million for the first Barack Obama-Mitt Romney encounter, 65.6 million for the second, and 59.2 million for the third. If Obama loses the election, it may be because he was listless in the first encounter and barely there in the third, thereby allowing his weak and vacillating opponent to catch up to him in the polls within days.

Several reasons have been proffered for Obama's failure at such a crucial moment, despite his brilliance, command of detail and personal integrity and discipline.

It's said that he does not relate to ordinary Americans, the way Bill Clinton and Ronald Reagan did. That he is an elite intellectual who does not enjoy getting down and dirty with opponents. That he got thrown off in the first debate by Romney's aggression — "probably no one has talked to him like this since his election" in 2008, said CNN's David Green, former adviser to four presidents.

Or that Obama is just fed up with the Republicans' extreme partisanship, their brazen distortions of his record and their own flip-flopping on key domestic and foreign issues.

Tough, say the critics. American elections are not a gentlemen's joust but rather bruising battles where winning, by hook or by crook, is all that matters.

There's also the economy, stupid. No American president wins presiding over high unemployment. Never mind that Obama inherited a mess and has put the economy on its way to recovery.

Still, it boggles the Canadian mind that the American electorate would take Romney seriously, despite all his inconsistencies, empty Cold War rhetoric and dedication to the same catastrophic economic prescriptions as George W. Bush's.

Half the electorate doesn't seem bothered as to how Romney would balance the budget while planning to spend $2 trillion more on defense and giving away $5 trillion in tax cuts, mostly to the wealthy.

Not just the Tea Party types but tens of millions more have been sold the lottery dream that they, too, can get rich like Romney and Co. if only the government got out of the way and taxed less.

And that the way to gut government is to hand it over to a guy who made a success of the 2002 Winter Olympics in Salt Lake City by taking a $400 million federal subsidy, and *whose running mate, Paul Ryan, is attacking Obama's $90 billion alternative energy program after milking it for his home state.*

And that the way to create jobs is to hand over the reins to the man who shipped jobs to China.

And the way to solve the crisis of 46 million people having no medical care and tens of millions more having the barest minimum insurance is to kill Obama's universal care and bring in vouchers for even more privatized care.

And the way to help the 47 per cent who don't pay taxes and whom Romney holds in disdain is to have them at the mercy of the generosity of the rich. As related by Ryan, didn't Romney tell a fellow-Mormon whose two kids were paralyzed in an auto accident, "I know you're struggling — don't worry about their college; I'll pay for it"?

Half of Americans couldn't care less about the other half.

Nearly half are committed Republicans and the other half Democrats. So it doesn't really matter if Romney moves from being a pragmatist to a "severe conservative" committed to extreme right positions on abortion, contraception, immigration, etc. to now, suddenly, pivoting back toward the centre.

In foreign affairs, the transformation is even more startling. After months of warlike noises, he's now a man of peace.

He does not want to bomb Iran, of course not. He does not want to send troops to Syria, does not even want to use American planes to enforce a no-fly zone there.

He agrees with Obama's pullout from Iraq, agrees with the pullout from Afghanistan in 2014, and supports Obama's increased use of drone attacks on Pakistan. He does not want a trade war with China.

Would a Romney be electable in Canada? To ponder that is to ponder the remaining differences between America and Canada."

Posted by Paul Rux, Ph.D. at 10:04 AM

Topic 35: Young Males in Ontario Today

We have made buying and selling a shibboleth: the customer is always right! NOT! But this is the absurdity that has arisen from making everything a transaction rather than a conversation or could we hope for a meaningful dialogue?

 An interesting discussion has arisen here in Ontario about young males who tune out in school. One teacher has suggested that video games give power to the player and they are frustrated when they enter an environment where they are not the controller. Unfortunately they are too immature to recognize that they can't always be in control.

 The other theme is that often parents' model bullying by harassing educators. Even twenty years ago some parents came to school consultations with lawyers.

 Finally, there are 'Christian' parents who are suing because they want to have detailed lesson plans for every lesson in advance so that they can keep their kids away from potentially hazardous 'education'.

 We've got a lot of teapot fascists running loose,

walter

Topic 36: American Cultural Pollution of Canada

Hi Paul,

Oswald Spengler observed that 'democracy' was matched to 'capitalism'. Mass production matched to mass movements, but the movements were manipulated in the interests of the monied elite. When I hear the rhetoric about taxation and the 'discipline of the market' I can't help but think that he was right. The rules of the game have been written by the 'owners'. Pro sports are an interesting analogy since there millionaires are butting heads with billionaires. The gladiators in the NHL want 50%# of revenue but the owners balk at that. Imagine if workers-Joe Plumber- got 50% of revenue. Until we sort our tangled notions of economic 'freedom' we really can't get to the main issues.

Even more basic is the question of freedom. As an undergrad, Eric Fromm framed the issue of freedom for me by distinguishing between freedom **from** and freedom **to**. We define liberty in terms of freedom from various things, but the bigger challenge is what we will do with the freedom we so generously enjoy- freedom to do what? This gets very personal. If you have free time, what do you do with it; if you have money what do you do with it.........It's not really the economy, stupid, it's what you do with the economy, stupid. In the past we were prepared to imagine great projects for the public good, now we have difficulty saving land for public parks. Our houses are oriented towards private backyards not the common street. In Barrie the health of a street is seen by whether the kids play there. Worse still, in the USA a very high % of all new housing is gated. Clearly this is a sign of a distrustful society- like the stockades on the frontier.

The barrage of fear generated by TV (the best measure of how fearful people are is the hours of TV they watch) and other media for profit is a great danger. Lazy 'news' scans the internet for related jolts when a situation arises in a community. A pedophile is caught in Britain and immediately all the pedophiles in the world are related to the story and it looks like an epidemic, when in fact sexual crimes were just as common in the past. Even the subtext in old movies where the language is very polite, indicates lots of domestic violence in the past. To me this miasma of American media- Fox news and the dumbing of popular culture for advertising $s is the greatest threat America poses for Canada. When you breathe polluted air you eventually get sick.

The tectonic shifts that are re-shaping civilizations need fearless and prescient leaders but I don't see them in the West. We are a fraction of what we were a 100 years ago in geography and demographic size, but much greater in influence through economic and cultural power. Our message of freedom, democracy & human rights belies our self-interested action in various military actions so we are gradually losing our credibility just as we have lost our physical size. I think that this leaves us with the choice to be good people ourselves and to try to make our immediate surroundings better. If enough people do this, life will get better.
We need to stay involved but take care of first things, first.
Cheers,
W

Topic 37: Bullying of Teachers by High School Kids in Canada

Dr. 123, I just finished grading ABC assignments, and the parallel XYZ assignments for the same students. These, as you know, are doctoral courses. Grading has become stressful after the university humiliated me because a student complained that I asked her to follow directions. The student threatened to drop out; the result was it was easier to humiliate me than to maintain standards. I actually had to apologize to her in front of six other staff and faculty for simply asking the student to follow directions. I experienced this in high school with teenage whining to guidance counselors. Now the whining has found its way into what once was higher education. We read and hear about bullying of students constantly, ad nauseam. Let's take a good hard look at the bullying of teachers by students today because of the desire to maintain enrollments at any cost and make money at any cost. Kiss standards good riddance.

You are afraid to enforce stated directions because you, the teacher, come under attack, not the student for not measuring up to meet simple assignment requirements. This is what we have come to. Tonight, I graded assignments; the stress of it has caused me to reach out to you for some relief, since you know full well of what I speak. It is time to find the exit door, save my health, and let the rotted game destroy itself. Fight or flight. I vote for flight. You cannot fight the system. Get out and away from it. When high school kids bullied me through guidance counselors I decided it was time to become a librarian. I have come full circle; it is time to exit for research pastures.

Posted by Paul Rux, Ph.D. at 8:03 PM

Topic 38: Immigration Offsets Prolonged Adolescence in Canada

Mark, if this is the case, we are wasting billions of dollars on prolonged adolescence in high schools. If K-12 does not hammer skills into students good and hard - the essence of educational Essentialism, the educational philosophy of this writer, not sentimental psycho-babble - we are wasting our money. This writer would oppose subsidies for such catch-up programs. Apprenticeships that do not require basic academic skills are the option for those who will not learn. This has been the essence of the European systems, which have not had "gazillions" of dollars to waste on babysitting. Third World countries are even more pressed to get return on investment, ROI, from their scarce dollars and do not put up with the adolescent antics that our K-12 tolerates. Do not worry. The crashing economy will sort things out. We do what we can afford. When we cannot afford it, it stops.

Canada relies on immigrants with hard skills, work ethics, and intact families to make up for the lack of discipline in its K-12 educational systems. At some point, the immigrants will tire of paying for the prolonged adolescence of their neighbors. In this, there is hope for Canada to avoid US model.

Posted by Paul Rux, Ph.D. at 8:03 PM

Topic 38: Immigration Offsets Prolonged Adolescence in Canada

Mark, if this is the case, we are wasting billions of dollars on prolonged adolescence in high schools. If K-12 does not hammer skills into students good and hard - the essence of educational Essentialism, the educational philosophy of this writer, not sentimental psycho-babble - we are wasting our money. This writer would oppose subsidies for such catch-up programs. Apprenticeships that do not require basic academic skills are the option for those who will not learn. This has been the essence of the European systems, which have not had "gazillions" of dollars to waste on babysitting. Third World countries are even more pressed to get return on investment, ROI, from their scarce dollars and do not put up with the adolescent antics that our K-12 tolerates. Do not worry. The crashing economy will sort things out. We do what we can afford. When we cannot afford it, it stops.

Canada relies on immigrants with hard skills, work ethics, and intact families to make up for the lack of discipline in its K-12 educational systems. At some point, the immigrants will tire of paying for the prolonged adolescence of their neighbors. In this, there is hope for Canada to avoid US model.

Topic 39 - Canada Shares Juvenile Consumer Culture with US

Walter, we share the same opinion about war. A profound study of the relationships between mindless consumerism and militarism in the USA is *The Limits of Power* by Andrew Bacevich. He correlates "good and hard" the directly cause and effect between mindless consumption of resources and military adventures abroad to steal resources to maintain this "shop -to-you-drop" culture. He is a retired senior US military officer who now teaches at Boston University. He is no amateur. He is also amazing because his extended military service has not cramped his ability to think clearly, logically. Yes, in effect, we have an adolescent culture that wants free stuff without having to work for it, an adolescent culture that no longer understands concepts like duty and limits - basic to classic Conservative thought. As you observe, the materialistic, juvenile culture is degenerate, and it will destroy itself.
Take care. Paul

Topic 40 - Educational Standards Crisis and Jobs Crisis

From first-hand experience as a high school teacher in Ontario, Canada, this writer knows that the same erosion of educational standards in the US is underway in Canada. This is why the US and Canada need immigrants with hard skills, work ethics, and intact traditional families.

Mark, this is first-class, thought, thorough, and very timely. In particular, your observation about how higher learning is moving away from degrees toward continuing education, also known as workshops and skill certificates, is exactly what MIT economist Lester Thurow predicted in his 1995 *The Future of Capitalism*. Thurow argued that nobody more and more knows what a degree means, if anything. How much knowledge and skill mastery does it represent, for instance? As a result, employers, the marketplace - as he predicted - is turning away from degrees toward training and development. In short, we have a jobs crisis because in large part we have a standards crisis. This is why your humble servant here belongs to ASTD, the American Society for Training and Development. Look to, prepare for the future. Great job!

Topic 41 - Thank God for the Canadian Example

Erik, wow, yes, dentistry is a key measure of social health. In the past, I have taught in one of the poorest counties in Ontario, Canada, Wiarton District High School. Fully a third of our students of a student body of 300 came from three nearby Indian reservations. Anyway, the absence of dental care hit you "right between the eyes" as a measure of the economic health of the area. During the Great Depression folks did not know there was a Depression! Nothing changed for them! Yes, your humble servant here is ardent about proper care for all - without bankruptcy. Canada's single-pay system works. I lived in Ontario for eight years. You cannot tell me otherwise. Recently, I told one of my old teaching friends in Ontario by email that yes thank God for Canada. It is living proof of what fairness is and how it works.

Topic 42 - Canadian and Wisconsin Progressive Values

Walter, Amen, Amen, Amen. One of the reasons why I love Canada dearly is its fairness. It factors fairness in its policies. This Republic does not any longer. It is time to restore fairness, the Progressive tradition here. What is amazing is Mt. Horeb, WI where we live is the hometown of Robert M. La Follett, the great Progressive at the turn of the 19th century into the 20th century. Is this some kind of fate, destiny? La Follett stood for fairness, US style; your humble servant here, in fact, grew up in this tradition. La Follett, for example, opposed US entry into WWI, rightly so. I recall walking in the park at night in Wiarton pondering on how I got there. My mind went back to La Follett and his stance for justice. Canada has had the advantage of the British connection, and with it cam acceptance of the NDP, UK Labor tradition as legitimate. Here the Wall Street vampires shouted down such stuff as un-American, anti-American. The USA has paid a price for it natavistic   break with the UK and Europe. Anyway, I wholly concur with the Holy Scriptures, which I seek to honor in my life. Yes, we are accountable in the final analysis. I hope I am a sheep, not goat. I need to get to bed after completing module 7 of 8 for the online university course, for which I am under contract. Thank you for your health considerations for me. I have noted them, and I have said to Jane I need some down time over the weekend. Anyway, I stand in the Progressive tradition. I recall reading the autobiography of E.C. Drury at U of T, who was a great Canadian Progressive. He lived in Barrier. His autobiography was *Farmer Premier*, if my memory serves me tonight. As I type this, I think of Simcoe, Barrier, Ontario, Canada, you and your family. You are blessed to live where you are. Meanwhile, I must weigh my duty here. Yes, as you observe, we are called. I want fairness here. Thank God Canada exists as an example of this fairness. It proves it can be done, starting with medical care for all. Thank you for the dialog. It is bedtime, now, for your old friend here in Mt. Horeb, Wisconsin, hometown of Progressive Robert M. La Follett. Paul

Posted by Paul Rux, Ph.D. at 11:36 PM

Topic 43 - Future of Prolonged Adolescence in North America

Jeanine, your concern is absolutely valid. Industrial psychologists tell us the average American today does not reach emotional maturity until age forty! Yes, we have a prolonged adolescence with no demands on people to grow up, contribute, accept responsibility, and embrace living beyond video games. In fact, young women in their early twenties have told me that they have a hard time finding potential husbands because of this prolonged childhood in our society. They said often their friends would consider marrying a man in his forties with emotional maturity. This is a sad, sad comment on our society. However, the coming Depression will wipe out the resources that support this extended adolescence good and hard. We will not be able to afford prolonged adolescence much longer. You are right. Dr. Rux

Topic 44 - Butterflies in Wiarton, Ontario, Canada

Brian, thank you for sharing this. One of the most creative teachers I known, worked with was in Wiarton, Ontario, Canada, at the high school, where I taught with him for four years. He was the geography teacher. He had kids make maps of our area, at the base of the Bruce Peninsula, which separates Lake Huron from Georgian Bay. After they made the maps, he arranged for them to go to the local airport and go up in a small plan to see how their maps compared with what they saw!

Of course, the principal of our school, D.H. Nickel, now deceased, RIP, saw the creativity in his geography teacher and gave him scope to exercise it! I can go on and on with more examples. The teacher ended up in Wiarton because when he taught in Ottawa, Ontario, Canada, the nation's capital, he was a threat to the "cogs in the machine" in charge and peers. He came to Wiarton. It was the classic "Butterfly Effect," based on the theory of complex numbers, which states: change occurs on the edges, not at the center. Amen. This teacher is now retired; he even wrote his own course textbooks - or manuals - and supplemented them with photos that he took on his jaunts literally around the world every summer! He had no car so he could do this traveling! On our last visit, he told how he had taken a group of students to the Arctic Circle, literally, to visit with and live in an Eskimo village! Learning geographic, physical and cultural does not get better than this. I have met nobody his equal since. Paul

Topic 45 - Conservative Americans and Canada

Walter, I am blessed to live in the hometown of the great Wisconsin/American Progressive Robert M. La Follett. He was one of the great Progressives here, as you may know. He believed in, worked for "open government," which is sadly lacking here now. I grew up on the Progressive tradition, heritage of my home state, Wisconsin. America, and sadly Wisconsin, too, my home state, badly need to return to recovery of its Progressive tradition. Is it an "act of God" that I have returned to these roots? I remind my friends here that we are heirs to La Follett, and the Progressive tradition, heritage, values, We ought to have the courage to preserve, apply, and transmit our heritage forward, now, again, in a second Progressive movement, which this hurting Republic so badly needs now. When I lived in Wiarton, Ontario, Canada, I often reflected on La Follett, for he, rightly, opposed the entry of the USA into World War I. Opposition to unjust wars is part of my Wisconsin heritage; it is amazing that I am now living in the hometown of this great Wisconsinite. Yes, I am truly Conservative at heart, as defined by Edmund Burke. Value, affirm, and transmit the values of the past forward. I have acted in the tradition (Burke again) of La Follett, and it is really, really ironic that now I am living in his hometown, at "ground zero" of this great Wisconsin value, contribution to this Republic. Keeping Faith with the past is the definition, essence, heart of Conservatism as it is historically understood. Yes, your old friend here in his own way is keeping faith with his heritage; Canada, God bless it, also keeps faith with the same heritage too!

Topic 46 -Old Ontario Keeps Calling

Walter, in 2013 Jane and I need to get out butts over to Ontario so we can visit with you and D-K in person, live, face to face. It's been too long. Thank you for keeping in touch, sharing your wisdom, and your friendship. You are the best. Meanwhile, the Republic teeters along. Jane and I will vote for Obama and the rest of the Democrats. We believe in fairness; the Wall Street gangsters control even more of the Republicans than they do of the Democrats. Besides, we need our Social Security and Medicare now. People here are somber. You see few bumper stickers, yard signs, buttons, etc. They know the "wheels are coming off the wagon" and the gangsters on Wall Street and their stooges in Washington - despite the horrific economic damage here, which is still mounting. The American people overall are good people when they remain true to their historical values. I make no apology for the "old time religion," for it brought me to Canada. The Pilgrims, New Englanders believed in the sanctity of "Conscience" bit time; it became my heritage too. Canada today is where America was in the 1950's. It is a sane, balanced place yet; people there still have a sense of optimism that is sadly missing here. The best part is Canada remains a fabulous reminder of what once was here and could be here again! Thank you for the comparison.

Topic 46 - Old Ontario Keeps Calling

 |

I sorely miss the Great Dominion to our North. It preserves American "know-how" without the violence. I guess at heart I remain an old Loyalist, "old school," Conservative, in the true sense of the word, concept, cf. Edmund Burke, one of my heroes. Anyway, Elora, Ontario keeps calling me now. My old friends in Wiarton have been dying out; thankfully, Elora has emerged to start a new cycle for me. I love Old Ontario, its ways. God willing, I will establish ongoing connections with it; it is not far from Barrie!

God bless, Paul

Topic 47 - The Professional Road to the University of Toronto

Johnny, your humble servant here has earned two degrees in history, B.A. (British) and M.A. (Canadian). I had the good fortune to study with, under J.F.C. Harrison, from the UK, and one of the world experts on how working class education emerged in response to the Industrial Revolution! I am not kidding. Early in my career, it was my great, good fortune to receive a thorough grounding in the origins of adult education - its issues and dynamics. And, study of the educational response to the Industrial Revolution equipped this writer to better understand how we are now adjusting education - working class, adult learning - to meet the demands of the Information Age! In both cases, Industrial and Information, sociology adjusts to technology, applies it and creates new modes of learning.

Harrison was from Leeds, UK, but found his way to my alma mater, the University of Wisconsin - Madison. He later became homesick and returned to the University of Sussex, UK. Before leaving, however, he made sure this reader here received a graduate fellowship to do his M.A. at Toronto!

My M.A. at the University of Toronto built on my B.A. studies, for its focus was the response of Canada to the challenges of the Industrial Revolution in the mid-nineteenth century. In this case, I focused on a Founding Father of Canada, T.D. McGee, who clearly articulated the need for Canada to develop a "Knowledge Strategy" if it wanted to move forward, compete, and prosper. The point is this. History tells us where we have been. If we know where we have been, we can have a better idea of where we want to go - and how to get there.
The Canadians when I got to Toronto said, "Why study British history. It is already written. Switch to Canadian history. It remains largely unwritten." I switched; I have lived happily ever after!

We totally agree on the importance of historical studies; in fact, I am in the process of turning my Toronto M.A. thesis into a book! The best part of history is it does not change! It is always "timely." Forgive the pun there. There, you "hit home" with your defense of the value of history.

Topic 48 -Canadian Social Values Shape Perceptions of Reality

Johnny, yes, your humble servant here, also starts with axiology, not ontology or epistemology. We seek what we value. In other words, values make us deductive, selective in our pursuit of facts and our ways to know them. Strictly, in formal philosophy, we are supposed to start with reality, ontology, study it (epistemology), and then construct our values (axiology) from the science of it. In reality, most of the time it is axiology that leads the charge. Dr. Rux

Topic 49 - Can Canada escape Gresham's Law?

Albert Jay Nock observed in his *Memoirs of a Superfluous Man* that he had nothing to say or offer to a society in which all values are squashed except "Economism," the notion that you can reduce all values simply to money to the exclusion of all other values, standards. We are heirs to Nock. The good news from him is the first-rate people abandon the failing enterprises clogged with second-rate minds, talents, who have no idea what the venture, enterprise required to launch and what is required to advance its health. This is Gresham's Law, "bad money drives out good money."

The good news is the first-rate venture forward to create new, healthy, enterprises that provide value beyond simply making money any old way as long as you get more and more of it. We are heirs to Nock. What we have experienced is not new. We ought not to worry if we are superfluous to dying, decaying systems under the control of second and third-rate talent. We rather need to respect ourselves and invest our God-given talents in ventures that offer more than simply money grubbing, starting with self-respect. I love Nock and his "little Nocks." Paul

Topic 50 - Possible Spillover of Fervor for Religion from USA to Canada

Brian, historians Will and Ariel Durant observed in their classic *The Lessons of History* that when law and order break down we see people turn to religion and ethics as a way to "push back" against abuse. This describes exactly the situation in America. The governmental system, which orchestrates the legal system, works for the vampires on Wall Street. As a result, we expect ethics to push back against abuse. I am not optimistic about the power of ethics to "right" the ship alone. In the end, raw power, government, must come into play - or we live in a dream world. Paul

Topic 51 - News about the Future from Toronto

Jason, look for educational technology, e.g. simulations, which are cheap and self-paced to more and more displace teachers, professors. Digital technology has the capacity now to "automate" learning and relegate teachers to the role of facilitators more and more. Teaching is what somebody does to us. Learning is what we do for ourselves; what we do for ourselves in the final analysis has more lasting impact. Call it discovery learning if you need a theory, name for it. The teacher unions here in Wisconsin are already worrying about this looming trend; higher education will also embrace the trend. We are in short looking at "teacherless" education, one of the core workshops at the 2012 World Future Society in Toronto, which your humble servant here had the good fortune to attend. 2013 is in Chicago! Closer.

Posted by Paul Rux, Ph.D. at 10:28 AM

Topic 52 - Collapse of School Discipline in America, not Canada, Yet

Sadly, when this writer taught high school in the Province of Ontario he witnessed the collapse of discipline in the high schools there. It is one of the reasons why he left Canada. Canada is lucky. It can still import disciplined talent from countries like India to drive its economy. America has a similar need. Sad.y, Canada borrowed American educational fads instead of devising its own. The result is to "Americanize" Canadian education - to the harm of Canada overall and its future.

Your humble servant here agrees and disagrees with you. Yes, we ought not to expect the same outcomes for all students. If they cannot do math, they can take options like woodworking. However, once they are in woodworking or math this writer sees no reason to relax standards

Topic 53 - Canada, USA, Greece, and Rome

To what extent do America and Canada reflect Greek city states or the Roman Empire? The comparison of the two countries with classical models gives us insight into their futures today. Bob, ancient history provides a model, comparison. Think Greek city states. Think Roman Empire. The city states were decentralized, but they formed leagues, or networks to use today's language, to meet various needs, e.g. defense and trade. In comparison, the Roman Empire centralized to the point that it broke down. It was a factory model. The Internet is now making it possible to decentralize in the fashion of Greek city states - which provides flexibility and human scale, in comparison with the mammoth centralized urban sprawl of ancient Rome. The themes of history remain constant; Futurists employ such historical comparisons to help us to make better sense of trends today.

Topic 54 - Good News from Old Friend in Canada Now

Michael, are you in Canada? If you are, bravo! Please confirm your location. Here is my take on this. John Johnson, now deceased, the guidance counselor at the high school in Wiarton, Ontario, where I taught for four years, put it this way. "90% of us will always work for somebody else, so why not make the system fair to the 90%?" In effect, the system cannot run without the 90% – regardless of the "smarts" at the top. It is an outdated industrial model in which intelligence is at the top of the factory system and the rest of the folks are just extensions of assembly line machines, dumb animals, robots, and slackers. This is breaking down in the Knowledge Economy. Political rhetoric, as you observe, has not caught up with the emerging reset, yet. John was from Sudbury, the son of Swedish immigrants who worked in the mines there. John started in the mines, and when World War II came he became a gunner in a Canadian bomber based in England. After the war, he became a teacher, then a guidance counselor. He was a great mentor to me. He was a realist. John also pointed out that the myth that all of us can make it into the top 10% of the ownership class is an opiate that keeps the exploitation going. In fact, 90% of the people who "play the game" are doomed to lose it – regardless of how many self-help and guides to success books they read. Fortunately, the Knowledge Economy in time will break down the hold this greedy 10% have on resources and allow a rest of how we live, do business; hopefully if we use this rest well, it will result in a fairer system. Fair is now my guiding concept. We need to be fair to the 90% – who do the work, obey the laws, pay the taxes, and fight the wars; for all of this their supposed "betters" exploit and abuse them. The late futurist Herman Kahn predicted that in time the 90% would wake up to the reality of the "game" and "blow it up." As we approach institutional failure in the USA, we are moving toward Kahn's forecast.

Topic 55 - Canada - USA Comparison July 2012

My wife and I had the good fortune to attend the 2012 World Future Society Conference in Toronto at the end of July. We spent two weeks in Ontario prior to the vent, which included visits to our favorite places like Leamington, Fergus, Elora, and Saint Jacobs. We also overnighted in Windsor, Guelph, and of course downtown Toronto. In short, we had a chance to sample public feeling.

Compared with the USA today, where Americans are anxious because they know "the wheels are coming off" the system, the Canadians in Ontario with whom we interacted were calm, optimistic, in comparison with their American cousins. For example, Toyota planned to open 400 new jobs in it Woodstock, Ontario plant. Overall, we heard good news about Canada in Canada. It was a stark contrast with the doom, gloom, and foreboding about the future we left behind in Wisconsin.

The gang shootings in Toronto, of course, jarred with the overall calm of the Canadians with whom we interacted. It was frankly a relief to be away from the dread of impending doom in America that we left behind when we cross the Ambassador Bridge into Canada at Windsor. In fact, it was hard to come back to the depression that Americans rightly have about their country. They do not deserve what has happened to them; they know it. Canada is a vibrant reminder that countries do not have to cater to economic terrorists, engage in overseas wars for oil profits, and go without healthcare for all.

The Canadians whom we met were not aware of the difference in social psychology between them and their American cousins. My wife and I became aware; we thank Canada for its example. Americans need to look North to their Canadian cousins for lessons on how to nurture healthy systems - and not suffer economic and political terrorism.

Posted by Paul Rux, Ph.D. at 11:12 PM

Topic 56 - History and Trend Forecasting = Imagineering!

Jori, your humble servant here holds two degrees in history: B.A. in British (focus on Industrial Revolution) and M.A. in Canada (focus on Industrial Revolution). Therefore, he is always pleased when students mine the technique of historical analysis in trend forecasting for their own purposes. Futuring and History are the same process. Both imagine. We use evidence to image the past - which is no longer here. We use evidence to imagine the future - which is not yet here! My study of history was a superb training in imagination application - or "imagineering." At the time, I was not aware of trend forecasting as a discipline, for it was just starting to emerge. I am delighted to see the overlaps!

Topic 57 - Canada Has Not Dismantled Its Progressive Heritage

Charles, the "robber barons" have an equivalent today. We call them the Wall Street "banksters" or "vampires" who have sucked the blood out of our economy. We are still going to pay dearly for this economic terrorism. The gangster politicians in Washington have used taxpayer funds to bail out the corrupt banks, and not a single "robber baron" on Wall Street has gone to prison, except for Madoff, a token gesture. This is why we have a new definition of "justice" in America. It is "just us." The last time this happened was during the start of the 1900's. One response to the corporate gangsters was the Progressive movement, which called for regulation of business to protect society and unions to protect workers. The Progressives laid the foundation for Roosevelt's New Deal. This writer is proud to say he lives in the hometown of Robert M, LaFollett, one of the greatest Progressive leaders at that time - or ever. He saw that the two-party system in his day, as in ours, was / is corrupt. So he and others in this country formed a Progressive party to advance reforms. We are on the verge of a Second Progressive Movement as local people realize they must now protect themselves from the gangsters on Wall Street and in Washington. We are on the verge of history "repeating."

Last night your humble servant here in fact attended an organizational meeting here in LaFollett's hometown on "grassroot networks" to organize the foundation for a new Progressive Movement. He plans to engage with this Movement, for it requires public policy research and education. The research and education interest me, and this writer has no desire to organize a political party. Yes, we are moving into a time of "reset," and we can look to the first Progressives who pushed back against the "robber barons" of their day to establish, for example, regulation of utility costs to prevent power companies and phone companies from gouging the average person who needs such services to literally stay alive today. I am proud to say I served on an advisory board to the Wisconsin State Public Utility Commission for eight years. The Commission regulates phone rates, power rates, railroad rates, etc. to protect the average person, the middle class, from economic terrorism. LaFollett and the Progressive created this Commission. I am also proud to say that I now share the hometown of Robert M. LaFollett as my new hometown. At our meeting last night I reminded the others of the "spirit" of LaFollett and how our Progressive heritage calls us to duty once again. Dr. Rux

Posted by Paul Rux, Ph.D. at 7:55 PM

Topic 58 - Canada and American Institutional Failure

How will the very real risk of institutional failure in the USA impact Canada? Look for a surge of refugees heading north for safety, stability, protection, and a productive life. How will Canada respond?

Matt, Alex Jones and others "sell tickets" through extreme statements to grab your attention. On the other hand, this writer believes we are risking "institutional failure," a situation in which people lose confidence in the (not their) government. Then a vacuum opens; nobody knows for sure what steps into it? Germany had such a vacuum in the 1929-1933, because of the Wall Street vampires. Now fast forward to our time. The Wall Street vampires – and their political gangster allies in Washington – have created a $17 trillion debt, which they will fund with fake money. Enter financial collapse. Yes, we face unrest, civil war in the streets, and a police state response. The challenge now is to have reserves to get out of the way as best we can.

We are like dogs that face an approaching attacker. We can fight or flight. This writer is in the flight mode, the safety mode, and the keep your head down approach. We cannot save a system from destroying itself. The best we can do is avoid having the rubble fall on us. Meanwhile, we save our strength, our optimism, and our talents for – yes – the future. Joseph Schumpeter called it "creative destruction." We cannot fix this. As my hero Peter F. Drucker taught, "Starve problems and feed opportunities." Your love of the rural is one asset for staying safe that you have. Do not overlook it. Trust your instincts. In the end, it is better to put our Faith in God, not men. Paul

Topic 59 - News from the Future from Toronto

News from the Future

World Future Society Conference 2012 Toronto

By Paul Rux, Ph.D.

Once a year, the World Future Society, the leading practice group for experts on discovering likely future trends, holds a three-day conference. To it come 500-600 experts from all parts of the globe to share their foresights about what probably is coming down the "pipeline" to shape our futures.

As a Professional Member of the World Future Society, who has designed and teaches online courses about trend forecasting for doctoral students at Jones International University, this writer was eager to attend and "mine" the conference for "nuggets" about emerging trends likely to shape our future. I would like to "share the wealth" with you through quick summaries of some "nuggets of foresight" that "bubbled" to the forefront of discussion in various conference workshops in which I participated.

The first "nugget" comes from the one-day workshop on the future of education that "kicked off" the conference for me. First, education is reaching a "fork in the road" between "learning," what we do for ourselves, and "teaching," what others (teachers) do to us. Emerging learning technologies favor self-paced "learning" and promote a growing trend toward "teacher-less" education. In effect, learning technologies can "automate" more and more learning processes. What does this mean for school and college budgets in the future? Online learning is just the "tip of the iceberg" of this trend.

A second "nugget" comes from the day-two workshop on the likely future of higher education. Here is the "news from the future" about post-secondary education. It faces a likely 10% loss of students yearly now because of the growing student loan and lack of jobs crises. The question for us is: "At a 10% loss of students yearly, in what kind of shape will post-secondary education be in five years?" Likely the response from educators will be their standard "more" taxpayer funding. The U.S. already has $1 trillion in unpaid student loans, 40% of which persons over age 60 owe! At what point does this "bubble pop" and we start to embrace options like pay-as-you go apprenticeships for most.

A third "nugget" comes from the day-two workshop on policing. It featured a panel of frontline policing trend forecasters from New York City (20 years service), Denver (14 years service), and Houston (12 years service). Here in a "nutshell" is their "news from the future." We are facing a reset in policing. The panelists called it "nurturing neighborhoods." It is code for do-it-yourself policing.

As budgets collapse at local, county, state, and national levels of government, police will not have the resources to protect us. In effect, we are going to be on our own. Justice is becoming "just us." Imagine.

The big shots in Washington have money for Wall Street "bankster" bailouts and bonuses, bombs and bullets in the Middle East, but they care and have nothing for the American people. This is a sobering forecast. The panelists are veterans; they know where cuts in police budgets are leading. They forecast a growing trend toward "walled" and "surveillance" neighborhoods as one result.

A fourth "nugget" comes from the day-three workshop on economic development trends. It dovetails with the day-two workshop on trend forecasts for policing. As we move into the future, the greatest asset a community will have in the competition for jobs will be public safety – not tax rates, real estate, and taxpayer "give-away" loans and grants. Nobody in his or her right minds, especially the "knowledge workers" who must drive the emerging economy of the future, wants to live where people get shot on the main streets, gangs beat people on the main streets and state fair grounds – without meaningful consequences. Computer scientists can easily move from here to Waterloo, Ontario, the "Silicon Valley" of Canada where laws prohibit "concealed carry" of weapons. If job growth depends on public safety, and common sense knows this, what does this say about our future?

Paul Rux, Ph.D. (Wisconsin-Madison) lives in Mt. Horeb, Wisconsin. He has presented workshops at the Washington, D.C. conferences of the World Future Society and published in its journal, *The Futurist.*   Last year he was part of an online, global research group on the future of teaching trend forecasting for the European School of Business, Wiesbaden, Germany.

Topic 60 - What the Canadian 13% federal sales tax buys.

Evony, my wife just spent two weeks in Canada. On every sale there is an automatic 13% sales tax. Federal. What does this buy? One, it buys health insurance for everybody; small businesses, large businesses too, do not have this as a cost. This probably is one of the reasons why Toyota opened 400 jobs in the area where we were last week! It is also why GM invested $1.5 billion in expanded production in Oshawa, Ontario, to the north of Toronto while we were there. It also pays all of the bills for the government of Canada, which is not in debt. Ours has over $17 trillion in debt, and this is rising. I will gladly pay the 13% tax in exchange for healthcare for all and no inflation of the currency because the government prints fake money to pay its debts, which is the case here. This inflation by fake money causes prices to rise on food, gas, clothing, etc. The middle and lower classes pay for this fake money through higher prices. The small business in Canada is farther ahead than here. The USA should learn from its neighbor to the North.

Wall Street is making too much money the way it is here now to ever do something fair, sensible. Travel comparison is learning.

Topic 61 - Pow Wows on the Future in Toronto

Geoff, thank you for the excellent expansion of Module 8 with Assignment 8.3. It really raises the final work product of the course to a hefty doctoral level. As I reviewed it, I kept thinking that, yes, it is challenging; on the other hand, I cannot imagine a student who completes this not taking personal (intrinsic) satisfaction with hitting such a high level of synthesis and professionalism. I really must thank you for providing this finale!

While we were in Toronto, my wife and I always, if they are home, visit with our dearest friends. He was in grad school at U of Toronto for his Ph.D. when I earned my M.A. there. We have remained loyal, lifelong friends. Here is the point. He is head of science at York University, student body of 66,000, in suburban Toronto. He has 10,000 students in his science department.

Right now, they are revising the curricula to make it competitive as we move into the future. He was sharing with me how he is dealing with resistance to his concept of change. Wow, I was able to share the core nuggets of EDU782 with him to bolster him for the faculty meetings that he faced the next morning! Talk about field testing EDU782! I carefully underscored the core of EDU782 – be sure of your core values, your philosophy, before you go into the arena. Then stick to your philosophy, and you will rally others. He sees the emerging theme of Apps, although he does not call it this. He wants students to have a skill-based curriculum that will enable them to constantly learn, unlearn, relearn, etc. as the future emerges! He was in effect doing a future trend analysis big time right there, but he did not have the concept to sum it up. I provided it.

I must share this because of how our private – the women were in the other room catching up – pow wow underscored the value of our work too. One, he validated the important of future studies, trend forecasting as crucial today. Two, he validated the philosophical foundation for leadership in the emerging – going into the future – age. He is a scientist, so he did not have the management science language, conceptual framework to provide the succinct summaries that future studies can.

The great part of it – besides having face-to-face time with a dear, old friend – was all of this happened as I was getting ready to attend the World Future Society conference that week in downtown Toronto. I am so very very pleased that JIU is embracing these best of the best practices that I have put forward for course development – futuring and philosophical foundations for leadership.

Our students are ahead of the "game" because of the JIU capacity to innovate; your polishing of these courses with me speaks to your "strategic foresight," to use a futuring term. Yes, I am so very pleased with our directions this year with course development.

The World Future Society conference was stunning! I even received an invitation to the annual conference of the Future Studies Society in Azerbeijan! Yes, it was a global conference, literally. I look forward to the next steps. Paul

Topic 62 - How does Plato apply to Canada today, its future?

Erik, as the late American philosopher Russell Kirk put it, we never learn anything new. We simply relearn. It seems each generation, some more than others, must relearn the lessons of reality. Today, your professor burdened his wife with an application of Plato's "cycles of government" from his classic study *The Laws*. Simply, Plato observed that self-control is always better than external controls. When people lose self-control because they abandon time-tested values, society reaches a point where it has a choice: collapse into anarchy and risk conquest, or restore order good and hard through a dictatorship. If we continue to unravel, degenerate, we risk reaching this fork in the road: collapse or dictatorship. Plato noted that external control is always of poorer quality than internal self-control. Sadly, the Macedonians conquered Greece shortly after Plato's death; Aristotle, the pupil of Plato, became the tutor of the future Alexander the Great! Aristotle "went with the flow" and accepted the end of his country's independence. Greece did not recover its independence until the 1800's almost 2,000 years later. It can happen. How does Plato's analysis help us to better understand present trends and where they may be taking us? Are we following his model, scenario?

Topic 63 - Canada did not follow insane American deregulation of financial institutions

Canada, to its great credit, did not join the American stampede to deregulate financial institutions. This is why the banks of Canada today are solid, not "zombie" American banks, which are "dead but still walking." Sadly, the American people have not yet grasped they have "zombie" institutions.

Shaun, your humble servant here just read *The Lessons of History* by Will and Ariel Durant, a husband and wife team of historians, who are "giants" of 20th-century historiography. Their "Lessons" - published in 1968 - sums up what they learned about history and human behavior because of their 11-volume historical study of Western civilization that leads up to their "Lessons," the twelfth, final book in their definitive study of the history of Western civilization. Here is what they have observed. When government regulation of bad behavior is lax, non-existent, look for a growth in the emphasis in society on ethics and religions to fill this vacuum. Boomo, bango, bingo! This is exactly what has happened in the USA. We have stopped enforcing laws against economic terrorism; as a result, we have a renewed interest in ethics as a way to "fight back." It is amazing to see how accurate the Durants are with their assessment of human behaviors; trend forecasters would say, yes, their model is a valid, reliable way to test current trends today. Trend forecasting does utilize historical models as ways to test current trends and project probable, possible future scenarios.

When "ethics" and religion do not do the job, we can look for a swing back to governmental regulation, maybe even law enforcement and punishment of business vampires and their zombie political allies. Durants suggest this could be the pattern in the future, for it has been the pattern in the past.

Editor/author Paul Rux, Ph.D. (Wisconsin-Madison), M.A. (Toronto) now lives in Wisconsin:

405 Lake St., Mt. Horeb, WI 53572.

Email: paulrux@hotmail.com

Phone: 608-471-2229

TOPIC INDEX

Topic Order Number	Topic Content	Topic Order Number	Topic Content
1	Terrorism	21	Latin America and Future
2	2016 U.S. Election	22	Canada equals USA.
3	Old School Ties	23	Canada does not equal USA.
4	Great Lakes Union	24	USA Gun Crazies
5	Walden Pond, Ontario	25	Great Lakes Nation
6	Future of Religion in Canada	26	U.S. Educational Trends
7	Canadian $ and IQ	27	Branch Plants
8	Model Toronto Professor	28	Bullying of Teachers in Ontario R&D
9	Education to Compete	29	Ontario Education
10	Rights, No Duties	30	Iran War
11	Union Busting	31	"One Nation Tories"
12	Natural Resources	32	"Thanatos"
13	Hometown Ontario	33	Happy Canada
14	Future of Religion in Canada	34	USA vs. Canada
15	Brazil and Future of Canada, USA	35	Young Males in Ontario
16	U.S. Tourism Down in Canada	36	Cultural Poison
17	Toronto Futurism	37	Teacher Bullying in Canada
18	Oxford in Canada	38	Immigration to Canada
19	"Lean" Learning	39	Juvenile Culture
20	U.S. Educational Poison	40	Jobs Crisis

TOPIC INDEX

Topic Order Number	Topic Content	Topic Order Number	Topic Content
41	Healthcare	61	Future "pow wows."
42	Shared Values	62	Plato and Canada
43	Prolonged Adolescence	63	Canada and Banking
44	"Butterfly Effect"		
45	Conservatives		
46	Old Ontario		
47	U of Toronto		
48	Social Values		
49	Gresham's Law		
50	Religious Revivals		
51	Toronto Future News		
52	No School Discipline		
53	Greece and Rome		
54	Canadian Good News		
55	Compare Canada with USA.		
56	"Imagineering"		
57	Progressive Canada		
58	Institutional Failure		
59	Toronto Future News		
60	Healthcare Canada		